SCHOLASTIC

TRUE or FALSE

Mammals

BY MELVIN AND GILDA BERGER

ISBN 978-0-545-20206-0

10 9 8 7 6 5 4 3 2 1   11 12 13 14 15

Printed in the U.S.A.   40
First printing, January 2011
Original book design by Nancy Sabato
Composition by Kay Petronio

Mammals are among the most popular pets.

TRUE OR FALSE?

TRUE! Mammals, Such as dogs and cats, are the most popular pets in the United States.

Most of us are also very familiar with farm mammals, which include pigs, cows, sheep, and horses. Millions of people visit mammals in the zoo — lions and tigers, monkeys and apes, bears and giraffes. Huge or tiny, tame or wild, mammals are familiar to almost everyone.

There are about 5,000 different kinds mammals in the worl

All mammals
live on
land.

TRUE
OR
FALSE?

FALSE! Many, but not all, mammals live on land.

Some, such as whales, dolphins, seals, and walruses, make their homes in the sea. Beavers and river otters are mammals that live in freshwater lakes and rivers. Most mammals that swim have bodies that are shaped like boats. This shape lets them move through the water quickly and easily.

Walruses' sensitive whiskers help them find food near the dark ocean floor.

All mammals have similar skeletons. **TRUE** OR **FALSE?**

TRUE! The skeleton of each mammal is basically the same.

Every mammal has a main backbone, or spine, to support the animal and help form its body's framework; a skull, to protect the brain and eyes; and ribs, to guard the heart and lungs. Then there are the limbs and connecting bones that allow the mammal to bend and move.

Mammals have the most complex skeleton of any animals.

Most mammals are born alive.

TRUE OR FALSE?

TRUE! Almost all mammals give birth to live babies.

The young are not hatched from eggs laid by the mother. Instead, they grow inside the mother's body until they are fully developed. In some mammals, such as kangaroos, the tiny babies are born before they are fully developed. They grow bigger in the mother's pouch until they can live on their own.

A baby kangaroo is called a joey.

No mammals lay eggs.

TRUE OR FALSE?

FALSE! Two kinds of mammals do lay eggs.

They are the platypus and the spiny anteater. The platypus mother lays her eggs in an underground nest and keeps them warm with her body. After the eggs hatch, the young feed on milk that oozes from the mother's skin. The spiny anteater keeps her eggs warm in a fold of skin on her body until they hatch.

Platypus and spiny anteater eggs have soft shells.

After they're born, mammals are helpless.

TRUE OR FALSE?

TRUE! Most newborn mammals cannot care for themselves.

Some are born blind, hairless, and completely dependent on their mothers. Others can see and hear, but they still need a parent to feed and care for them. A mammal's first food is milk from its mother's body. Mother's milk gives the newborn mammal all the nutrition it needs to grow bigger and stronger.

In a few mamma[l] families, father[s] help care for the[ir] young.

Sea mammals breathe underwater. TRUE OR FALSE?

FALSE! Sea mammals breathe air like other mammals do — they cannot breathe underwater.

They must come to the surface regularly to get a breath of air. The mammals draw the air into their lungs through their nostrils. Then they hold their breath for a long time. Some whales can stay underwater as long as an hour and a half between breaths!

Some female sea mammals, like the se lion, leave the wate to give birth.

All mammals
have hair
or fur.

TRUE
OR
FALSE?

TRUE!

All mammals have hair or fur, even if it's just a few whiskers. Hair keeps mammals warm. It also hides them from attackers by helping them blend in with their surroundings. Whales have almost no hair. Smooth, hairless bodies help them swim faster. Porcupines protect themselves with long, sharp quills that are really hairs grown together.

Rhinoceroses' horns are made of hair.

Mammals keep a steady body temperature. **TRUE OR FALSE?**

TRUE! A mammal's body always stays at about the same temperature — no matter the weather.

This is called being warm-blooded. A lot of a mammal's heat energy comes from the food it eats. Also, a coat of heavy fur allows some mammals to live in icy-cold lands. Feeding at night and resting in water during the day keep other mammals comfortable in very hot conditions.

Many mammals gain extra fat an grow heavier fur the winter to kee themselves warm

Mammals usually live alone.

TRUE OR FALSE?

FALSE! Many mammals live in groups rather than by themselves.

This is because living with others is safer. Some mammals, such as baboons, live in large groups called troops. The leaders, which are the biggest males, keep the group together. They warn members of danger and stop them from fighting among themselves.

The tiger is one of the few mammals that lives alone most of the time.

All mammals eat meat. TRUE OR FALSE?

FALSE! Cows and many other mammals usually eat plants.

These plant eaters are called herbivores. They have flat teeth to grind up the plants. Lions and some other mammals are meat eaters, called carnivores. They have sharp teeth to grab and hold their prey. And some mammals, such as bears, eat just about anything. Known as omnivores, many of these animals have both kinds of teeth.

Lionesses hunt together for prey t feed a pride, or grou of lions.

Bears find all their food on land.

TRUE OR FALSE?

FALSE! Many bears get food in rivers or the ocean, as well as on land.

On land, black, brown, and grizzly bears eat berries, fruits, and nuts. They often eat small animals, too, such as mice, squirrels, and ants. These bears also wade into streams to catch and eat salmon and other fish. Polar bears hunt seals, which they catch in the Arctic Ocean.

Polar bears usually cat seals when they come t the surface for air.

More mammals live in rain forests than anywhere else.

TRUE OR FALSE?

TRUE!

Tropical rain forests are home to more mammals — and animals overall — than any other habitat. This is because dense rain forests have huge amounts of plants available year-round for the plant eaters. And meat-eating mammals can feed on the many birds, insects, and other kinds of animals that live in the rain forest.

Rain forests now cov
about 6 percent of
Earth's land surface

Some herbivores eat only one kind of plant.

TRUE
OR
FALSE?

TRUE! A number of plant eaters eat just certain plants, or parts of one kind of plant.

Giant pandas are especially fussy. They like only the shoots, leaves, and stems of the bamboo plant. Koalas are also very particular about what they eat. All of their meals consist of leaves from eucalyptus trees.

Giant pandas ea[t] 20 to 40 pound[s] (9 to 18 kilogra[ms]) of bamboo a da[y].

All mammals sleep at night.

TRUE OR FALSE?

FALSE!

Quite a few different kinds of mammals sleep all day and are awake all night. They are called nocturnal mammals. Nocturnal mammals come out at night to seek food. The darkness helps them hide and escape from predators. Mammals that are more active at night than during the day include opossums, skunks, and jaguars.

Mammals that sleep at night and look for food during the day are diurnal mammals.

Many nocturnal mammals have big eyes or ears.

TRUE OR FALSE?

TRUE! Nocturnal mammals have especially good senses of sight or hearing.

Many have eyes or ears that seem almost too big for their bodies. Large eyes help tarsiers and other mammals find food in darkness or dim light. Big ears help fennec foxes hear prey that they cannot even see.

Most nocturnal animals have very good senses of smell.

Bats are the only mammals that can fly.

TRUE OR FALSE?

TRUE! Bats are the only known flying mammals.

Each bat wing is made up of thin skin stretched over the bones of the bat's arms, fingers, and legs. Only its feet are not covered with skin. Wings let bats fly and find food in the air that other mammals cannot catch or reach.

Some bats can fly up to 2 miles (3.2 kilometers) high.

The elephant
is the biggest
land mammal.

TRUE
OR
FALSE?

TRUE! Elephants are the world's biggest land mammals.

There are two kinds: the Asian elephant and the heavier, taller African elephant. The Asian elephant has smaller ears than its African cousin does, and only the males have large tusks. Both male and female African elephants can have large tusks.

A male African elephant weighs about as much as four midsize cars

The mouse is the smallest mammal.

TRUE OR FALSE?

FALSE! The Kitti's hog-nosed bat takes the prize as the smallest mammal in the world.

It is small enough to fit in the palm of your hand, with a wingspan of only 6 inches (15 centimeters). It also weighs less than a penny — just half an ounce (2 grams).

The Kitti's hog-nosed bat is sometimes called the bumblebee bat.

Cheetahs are the world's fastest mammals.

TRUE OR FALSE?

TRUE! Cheetahs are the fastest of all mammals.

Their high speed lets them race across the plains of Africa and catch the swiftest prey. Thanks to their streamlined bodies, long, powerful legs, and sharp claws that grip the ground, cheetahs can reach speeds as high as 70 miles (112 kilometers) per hour — but only for short distances.

Long ago, human hunters trained cheetahs to catch smaller animals.

Many mammals live in the desert.

TRUE OR FALSE?

TRUE! Many mammals are equipped to live in dry, sandy conditions.

Small desert mammals get all the water they need from the seeds, shoots, or animal prey they eat. Larger desert mammals, such as wild camels, can survive for many days without water or food. They usually try to stay out of the daytime heat to keep cool and save water.

Camels store fat, not water, in the humps their backs.

Humans are mammals, too.

TRUE OR FALSE?

TRUE! Humans are mammals, just like elephants, dogs, cats, and hippos are.

All of us have backbones and similar skeletons. We develop inside our mothers' bodies. Human mothers can nurse their babies with milk from their bodies. We're warm-blooded, have hair, and breathe air. Aren't mammals fascinating?

For their size, humans have larger brains than any other mammals do.

Index